VOICES FROM THE LAND

FREE RIVER PRESS
FOLK LITERATURE SERIES

Robert Wolf, General Editor

VOICES FROM THE LAND

Selected and Edited
by
Robert Wolf

FREE RIVER PRESS

ISBN# 1-878781-05-7
© by Free River Press
All rights reserved

Free River Press
RR 2, Box 96
Lansing, IA 52151

First printing: October, 1992
Second printing: November, 1992

This book is made possible through
the generosity of the
Lynn R. and Karl E. Prickett Fund

CONTENTS

Foreword by Robert Wolf.............................. page 1

PART I: BEFORE DIESEL
Memories by Richard Sandry...................... page 4
Threshing by Richard Sandry .... page 8
Meals for Threshers by Clara Leppert ..... page 10
Home a Hotel by Clara Leppert................. page 12
Horses vs. Tractors by Barb Leppert......... page 15
Our Farm by Frances Geinzer .... page 17

PART II: FARMING TODAY
Farming by Bob Leppert .... page 20
High Interest Dilemma
   by Barb Leppert .... page 26
Getting Started by Essie Welsh.................. page 28
The Coming of Machinery
   by Barb Leppert .... page 31
Would You Believe It?
   by Richard Sandry..................................... page 33
Forced Auctions by Greg Welsh................ page 35
Farm Crisis by Greg Welsh......................... page 36
The Tornado by Frances Geinzer .... page 37
Bluebirds by Dorothy Sandry .... page 40

PART III: LAND STEWARDSHIP
Soil by Bruce Carlson .... page 44
Image of Farmers by Essie Welsh.............. page 47
The Day the Welsh Family Farm
   Turned Around by Bill Welsh............... page 49
The Way Back by Greg Welsh.................... page 54

FOREWORD

This book, most of which was written by Lansing, Iowa farmers in a writing workshop under the auspices of Free River Press, was intended to give these farmers and other participants a platform from which to air their views on the impact of technology on farming practices, the land, and the community.

At first there were seven of us, three farming couples – Bill and Essie Welsh, Bob and Barb Leppert, Francis Geinzer and Danny Cole, and myself. Danny dropped out but Greg Welsh, Bill and Essie's son, Clara Leppert, Bob's mother, and Bruce Carlson, the Lansing dentist, joined us. Others came by briefly, among them Dorothy and Richard Sandry.

We began meeting shortly before Christmas 1991, and met every Monday after evening chores, rotating from one farm house to another, until spring planting. For me it provided community; perhaps for the others, too. Certainly they anticipated each week's meeting, not only for the writing and the reading and the reactions they got to their work, but for the socializing afterwards, when the hosts would bring out tea and coffee, sandwich makings or desserts. They called it lunch.

Over food and coffee we would discuss the loss of community, the decline of the national economy, the problems of the family farm, and ways to counteract the dissolution we saw everywhere. And I would think to myself, "If only some of my city friends could hear these conversations!" Without being there, they would find it hard to believe the level of sophistication. Besides, some of my urban friends had the most absurd views of rural life, considering it an aberration and their own frantic existence, sensible.

Most of us had separate agendas for the project. I had told the farmers that once each of them had finished a piece that we would give public readings with discussions afterwards in which they would be able to engage urban audiences, and that those discussions would be the heart of the project.

I anticipated that my neighbors would impress urban audiences, and they have. After their reading in LaCrosse, Wisconsin, a college professor remarked, "I thought people like that died out forty years ago!" He was impressed with their dignity and integrity.

I am extremely fortunate to live among them. Having resided in ten states, among all sorts and conditions of people, I have seldom met their like. They live the agrarian ideal that Jefferson wanted for this country: they are the virtuous citizens that he dreamed would fill the continent.

This book is a record of community that once existed here, of the growing costs and instability of farming, of the love of the land. It is their first anthology, but not their last. Keep in mind that it is folk writing, and merely skims the surface of what's to come.

ROBERT WOLF

Cover art by Bonnie Koloc

PART I:

BEFORE DIESEL

RICHARD SANDRY

Richard and Dorothy Sandry arrived at the workshop several months after it opened, recruited by Greg Welsh. Richard's facility impressed everyone, but Dorothy informed us that years ago he had written love poetry for her. That first evening he wrote a piece on threshing, then disappeared for the winter. Then, sometime in the spring, Richard unexpectedly arrived at my home, bringing this piece.

Memories

It stands alone now and largely unnoticed by the numbers of people who pass by it every day of their busy lives. Like a giant old oak tree that is removed from the scene, it would not really be missed, unless for some reason, one day, the building would be gone. Officially it was known as Lansing No. 3, but to most it was known as the Churchtown School.

Its life has been stripped from its interior: the students' desks, the teacher's desk, the recitation bench, and all the material that set it aside as a place of learning for those first wonderful eight years of elementary education. Its bell having rung to call the children to its doors for the last time some thirty-five years ago, its only purpose now is to serve as a monument of brick and mortar to by-gone days. Days of a slower pace of life, when terms like 'substance abuse,' 'AIDS,' 'government programs,' 'government deficits,' 'welfare programs,' and 'abortion' had not yet come into being.

Built in 1875 on the highest spot in the nearby area, it commands a panoramic view of the hills and valleys dotted by farms and homes. Some of the farms are now empty and their buildings mostly abandoned because, due to the government's cheap food policy, their owners could not make enough money to support their families and had to move on. These same farms in earlier times were prospering and sending sometimes six or seven children to school, all at the same time.

Due to the lack of records we have to use our imagination and fantasize that maybe the builders of the school somehow stored away a spirit in her. Maybe in the belfry or perhaps behind her two large blackboards. What stories she could tell of nature's elements beating against her walls like so many armies trying to knock down the walls of a fortress. For nearly one hundred and seventeen years she has won every battle, and stands as sound as the day of her completion.

She would remember her first teacher telling the students about then-President Ulysses Grant and of the Civil War and President Lincoln's assassination just ten years before.

She also heard firsthand of current events like the Spanish-American War, the sinking of the Titanic, the first automobile, the first airplane, World War I, the great depression, World War II, and the Korean War. The time span of fifteen presidents from Grant to Eisenhower.

I wonder if she would remember that first day of school in the late summer of 1941 when a shy, black-haired boy entered her door for the first time to begin his eight years of education. He soon learned the advantage of being the first one to school on those opening days in succeeding years, not because he was so anxious to begin the year, but because that usually gave him the pick of his desk for the year. The best one being the one by the window, where if the teacher didn't notice, he could look out of the window to see which neighbor was passing by with their team of horses or which one was going by with their new Farmall H or M or John Deere A or B tractor.

The old building would surely remember the students preparing for the Christmas programs for weeks before the big evening arrived. That evening all the parents and many others of the community would come to see the program of "pieces" and plays. The final instruction being to speak loud and clear so the people in back could hear. This was all followed by a gift-exchange and a two-week vacation.

She would remember the row of bicycles parked by her wall in the spring and fall and the coaster sleds in the winter time. Also the row of dinner buckets ranked in the hall waiting to be opened at noon and sometimes their contents traded or bartered for something in someone else's bucket. Also the large water cooler, which was filled every morning by two of the older boys going to the creamery with a can and bringing back the day's supply of drinking water. This was an enjoyable twenty-minute trip.

When nature called, the procedure was to raise one's hand and ask, "Teacher, may I leave the room?" Permission granted meant a trip of about forty yards to the outdoor toilet. Funny, but nature always seemed to call more often in the nice days of the spring and fall than it did when it was thirty below zero in the winter time.

Heat was furnished by the one large register in the middle of the floor, which also necessitated an outside trip to the side door to stoke the old furnace with coal. The last day of school in the spring was also a big occasion, as that day all of the mothers would pack the picnic basket with goodies and the fathers would stop their work long enough to come to school so everyone could enjoy the picnic dinner. After a few games were played, the parents would take the children home with them to begin the summer vacation. That day brought talk (with mixed emotions) of whether there would be a new teacher for next year.

Now back to reality. Fifty years have passed since that day in forty-one. The boy has grown to be a man, the black hair has mostly turned grey, and as he drives past the old school he looks into that same window, smiles, and says to himself, "Old school, thanks for the memories."

Threshing

by Richard Sandry

When you are ten years old and can be along with the men on the threshing crew, it can make you feel pretty grown up. The threshing ring then consisted of about twelve neighboring farmers.

Sometime in July when the oats fields were all a golden yellow, it was time to cut and shock the grain. The grain binder was brought out from its year of rest in the machine shed and was pulled by five strong horses, or in later years by a tractor. The fields then turned from yellow to a shade of green as the oats were cut, tied in small bundles, and deposited in rows on the ground by the binder. Usually this was done on some of the hottest days of the summer.

The oats bundles then had to be picked up by hand and shocked. A shock was usually six bundles set on the ground with one bundle laying horizontally on top, called the cap. Many farmers liked to do the shocking in the cool of the evenings, sometimes keeping on until midnight. For the next two weeks, the shocks went through a sweat, or drying time.

It was then time to begin threshing. Each farmer would bring his team of horses and his "basket rack," which was a large wagon box to hold the bundles. Some had tractors hitched to the wagons. It was necessary to move along the rows of shocks to load the wagon. This is where I came in as a tractor driver. This was a big help to the man who was loading the wagon, as he did not have to crawl continually on and off the tractor. To be able to drive those early tractors was quite a thrill for a young boy.

The bundle wagons were then brought, one on each side of the threshing machine, and the bundles pitched into the machine, one bundle at a time. The machine separated the oats from the straw, the oats coming out of a spout and put into sacks. The sacks of grain were then hauled to the granary where they were emptied. The straw was blown onto a pile which was called the straw stack.

Dinner was always something to look forward to. Three or four of the farm wives would go together and cook the noon meal. It was served family style with all of the men sitting around the table. When the men were eating, there was plenty of kidding and telling of tall tales, which really held my attention. I'm sure my dad did not share my enthusiasm for the threshing, as for him it meant a lot of hard and sweaty work, but for a ten-year-old boy it was the big event of the summer.

CLARA LEPPERT

Clara is the mother of Bob Leppert, and one of the people who gives this project its unique cast. She is eighty-four years old, a delicate yet lively woman with a style whose honesty and artlessness are a spontaneous reflection of herself.

Meals for Threshers

When the grain was ripe it was put in shocks, most people placing six bundles together and a bundle on top to keep the rain from soaking in. The grain was usually oats, sometimes it was barley, which was scratchy and made us itch. Afterwards, the dry grain was put in the huge threshing machine, which separated the kernels of grain from the straw. We expected sixteen to eighteen men when we threshed, and they worked from sunrise to sunset.

For many years Marie Fritz and I helped each other cooking meals. In the morning we would put a bench outside, and place two wash tubs of water on it, two or three basins, a couple of combs, and a mirror.

Some people gave lunch both forenoon and afternoon, the women taking it to the field. We took lunch only afternoons. We would take sandwiches, cookies or doughnuts, coffee and real homemade lemonade. Two or three days before threshing, we would bake two or three batches of cookies. Threshing day we usually had a big beef roast, mashed potatoes and gravy, two or three vegetables, cheese, and always two kinds of pie.

For supper we usually had meat balls, meat loaf, baloney or wieners, escalloped potatoes or potato salad, vegetables, cake, cookies, and sauce.

One time when Clarence was helping thresh at a neighbor's, they were served delicious clover blossom wine. It tasted like flavored sugar water, but after a little, the table began to go around; pretty soon it was going around so fast, it was hard to catch the food when it went by. After awhile, all was well again.

The next big group of men worked on silo filling, then corn shredding. As it got cold, the men got together again to saw wood. If one neighbor worked for another five days and the other one worked two days, there was never anything said about one owing the other.

Home A Hotel?

by Clara Leppert

Sometimes my home seemed like a hotel.

There were two homeless men who came often and would stay sometimes two or three weeks at a time. They would finally leave to go some other place for a little while but would soon be back again.

We were looking at pictures one night, when one of the men was here. Ruth, our daughter, was a beautiful young girl. We didn't know until a long time later that Myron put one of her pictures in his pocket and told people everywhere he went that she was his girlfriend.

We had a lot of agents that managed to come about noon. Every time I saw one was outside talking to the men, I put another plate on the table. It was easy to have one more, and we always had a nice visit.

One time Andrew Wacker was with us at dinner time; he emptied the horseradish jar. We thought he didn't know what he had, it was like a nice mound of mashed potatoes. He enjoyed it a lot it seemed, until the last mouthful.

The telephone repairmen asked if they could eat here. I would have five or six men three days in succession for the noon meal (for several years). They would pay 75 cents a plate. I saved the money and bought a used piano that I still have. When Clarence brought it from Waukon, the hill was very steep by the May's Prairie Cemetery, and he lost the bench. He realized it had fallen out and stopped for it. When the man carried it in the house, one of them said, "This piano is so heavy, you will find it in the basement one of these days."

Sometimes fishermen would stop in the morning, and ask if they could have a noon meal. They were always nice men, they wanted to pay a dollar each.

One time a bus full of prisoners worked down at the creek making hiding places for the trout. One of two men would stop in every morning for drinking water. They were all nice looking young men and I wondered why they were prisoners at Luster Heights. I felt sorry for them and each day gave them a three pound coffee tin of homemade cookies. Later a neighbor asked, "Did you let them in the house?" I didn't have any fear about it.

A couple of years later a man and a pretty girl came to the house. I recognized him at once as being one of the prisoners. He said, "This is my wife, I want you to meet her. I want you to know we appreciated all those cookies you gave us, and I want my wife to see where we made hiding places for the trout. Your neighbors were so good to us, they always waved when we went by. We worked near Decorah later, and they treated us just like prisoners."

I said, "Won't you tell us your name and where you live? I'd like to hear from you sometimes." He said, "We will stop on our way back from the creek." I said, "I will have lunch ready for you." The lunch waited and waited but they didn't stop.

I don't know how long three ex-soldiers stayed

here when they got back from the service, Art Swenson, John Fritz and Ronnie Haas. They needed good meals, and to think of other things than war.

I had young folks stopping in for meals a lot when my sons, Howard and Bob, were teenagers. One day it was supper time and three or four extra lads came to eat. One of them said, "I caught a turtle down at the creek, you can fix it for supper." I said, "I don't know how to cook a turtle." He said, "I'll tell you." I ate a little bit, just so I could say I'd eaten turtle.

If we weren't gone, we almost always had a group of people for Sunday dinner.

A German came to the neighborhood, we felt he had escaped prison. He was almost always angry. He would be here a month or more at a time, cutting wood. After he got up in the morning he would walk around the house five or six times screaming. I asked him what was the matter; he said in German, "God in Heaven, the devil for us all. I tell the whole world."

When he would be in the woods working, all of the neighbors could hear his sermons. I didn't feel it was safe to have him in the house, but Clarence felt it was all right, and we needed a lot of wood.

BARB LEPPERT

Barb is well respected in the community as a fourth-grade teacher. She works on the family farm as well, helping her son, Andy, with morning and evening milking. Like the others in the group, she has great resources. Her sketches help give readers an idea on the nature of daily farm life.

Horses vs. Tractors

The horses were already gone when I came to live on the farm, so I don't have any firsthand knowledge, but I have heard a lot of stories from my husband and his parents.

The horses were worked pretty hard for an hour or so, and then they had to be rested. The woman of the house, knowing this, could plan for the noon meal to be done to coincide with one of these rest periods. The horses were brought in and watered and fed, and only then would the men come in for their meal. They would sit down to chicken, mashed potatoes and gravy, corn on the cob, coleslaw, fresh baked bread (that you could smell all the way out to the field), and a big slab of juicy apple pie. After devouring this meal they would go outside under the big shade tree in the back yard, sit down in the lush green grass and tell stories or jokes until the horses were sufficiently rested.

In contrast, today, when I have dinner prepared and ready at noon, it might be 1 p.m. or later before Bob comes in, because he wanted to get that field finished or get all the hay raked so he could bale it later in the afternoon.

He hurriedly eats his dinner with one ear glued to the radio to get the latest weather forecast. No one dares to talk while he listens. If there is any rain in the area he jumps up, heads for the door, and gets back on the tractor that didn't need to be rested or fed anything but gasoline!

FRANCES GEINZER

One never knows whether Frances will show up in an Aussie bush hat or a scarf and earrings. For an Iowa farmer, her vacations are unusual, too. She has traveled to Australia at least once, and made several wagon train rides in South Dakota.

Our Farm

I have lived on the family farm all my life and have enjoyed every day of it. Our farm has been in the family for one hundred and thirty-eight years, being homesteaded by my great-grandfather and great-grandmother, Adam and Margretta Hirth. They cleared the land and raised a family. All farming was done with oxen and horses, while raising registered Aberdeen Angus cattle and Persian horses. Adam passed away at an early age, but the farm was run and kept together by Margretta. In time one of her sons took over and carried on, marrying and raising a family. At one time three families lived in the original log house, which still stands. It is all hand-hewn as is part of our one barn.

My father took over in 1918 when he married, and all went quite well in spite of low prices and expense, but then in those days what had to be bought was not so high and leveled with selling prices.

In 1932 father suffered a fatal heart attack and passed away, leaving mother with two daughters and a pile of debts. All of father's relatives who he had borrowed money from wanted their notes clear.

Daddy died without a will, leaving the whole farm at risk, and Mother could not pay it off, as those years were in the heart of depression times and we were very poor. The land was all taken from us and rented to some of the neighbors. Mother only had four acres, which was given her as a homestead. But my mother, my aunt, my sister, and me all worked hard and with the help of a good hired hand we rented land wherever we could to make feed so we could keep our livestock.

As time went on we bought land, but of the original three hundred and twenty acres Daddy had, we just got two hundred and twenty back. In later years I and my husband acquired our own land to add to Mother's, altogether making fourteen hundred acres. In the past years my mother, aunt, and husband all passed away.

At this time my second husband and I run the whole ranch. We have a cow-calf herd and a flock of sheep. So far all is going well. We both love the land and enjoy our work, so the Lord willing we can reap from a good and independent country life.

PART II:

FARMING TODAY

BOB LEPPERT

Bob was one of the first organic farmers in Allamakee County. He is a man who thinks and questions, and is open to experience. Most farmers resisted the invitation to the workshop, Bob found it intriguing. As someone noted about most of the group, they are striving to express ideas, not trying to be literary. Bob's work, like that of the others, is of a piece with the rest of his life.

Farming

The first farming I was able to do when I was growing up was to help take care of the chickens: feed them, get the eggs, and at night make sure they were all in the coop with the screen door closed so foxes couldn't get them. I was too small to harness the horses because the horses were so big. My brother was three years older than I and he could get them on by himself. Everything, the plowing, discing, and planting, was done by horses. We had our W-30 McCormick Deering tractor but it was only used for providing power to grind feed, thresh grain, and shred corn because we had all horse machinery at that time.

I can remember when planting corn, I would help move the planting wire for the planter. It had buttons on it and would be stretched all the way across the field to be planted. The planter had a guide to hold this wire while going across the field, and each one of the buttons would trip the planter to drop the corn in the ground, so that when we cultivated the corn, we could cultivate it the long way and also go across the field to help control the weeds.

Chemical fertilizers, herbicides, and insecticides weren't available yet. About this time, hybrid corn became available and would be standing in the fall when it was time to harvest. This was unreal, because the open pollinated corn seemed always to be laying on the ground. My hands would be so cold when we had to pick the ears out of the snow. I would keep asking if it was time to start chores so I could get to the house and warm up.

About this time we got our first rubber tire tractor, a two-cylinder John Deere B, with a brake for each rear wheel, which was really an improvement to help it turn in loose soil. This tractor would run on power fuel, which was similar to kerosene. The tractor had two fuel tanks, a small one to put gasoline in and a large tank to hold power fuel. When the tractor was cold it had to be started on gasoline and switched to power fuel when it was warmed up. I can remember the fuel man filling our fifty-five gallon tanks in the shed. There were no pumps on the truck and he filled five gallon cans and carried them in and emptied them in the tanks, each time moving a lever with numbers on the rear of the truck to keep track of the total amount of fuel delivered.

As each year went by, Howard and I would pester Dad to cut the horse tongues off the implements so we could use the tractor on them. Also, we kept buying more machinery as it became available after the end of World War II. In 1946 we purchased a new John Deere A tractor with a two-bottom plow and cultivator for $810.00. Then came the fifties and with it, chemical fertilizer, herbicides, and insecticides. I remember the first year we used a herbicide: the instructions were not followed correctly and we had corn that year, no weeds, but it was four years before anything else grew on it. We never did use any pesticides because we only had corn one year in a field, then it would be rotated to oats and then hay for the next two years.

In the fifties we purchased our first diesel powered tractor and a four-row corn planter and cultivator. During this time, the popular statement was, if you are having financial problems, get bigger. My brother and I would buy every calf and pig we could afford and then some. We would rent farmland even if we had to drive five miles to get to it. We worked day and night to get all the work done. We did this all through the fifties and sixties. By the time we got into the seventies we were so big we were having serious problems getting money to keep going. We had passed the limit at our local bank and were getting money through them from two other banks in the cities.

About this time we had grown with our cow-calf operation to two hundred and twenty cows. Then two farms we had been renting were put up to auction and we figured we couldn't afford to purchase them. The next year the State Conservation Commission notified us that it was terminating the leases on the land used to pasture our cattle. We were very disgusted and in the spring of '72 we took a hundred and fifty of the cows to the sale barn. As I look back now, it was the best thing that could have happened to us. The cattle sold good and we were able to lower the amount we had borrowed quite substantially at the bank. This was the first time we were able to pay off rather than borrow. We changed our cattle operation around and sold yearling calves rather than finish them out to fat cattle for slaughter. We found as we got smaller that our profits increased. Better efficiency meant less interest to pay at the bank.

About 1976 I got invited to a dinner meeting put on by the Wonder Life Corporation and got introduced to organic farming. There were a couple of farmers there who had been farming this way for years, but I couldn't believe that this could work, even though I thought it was a good way to farm. So I had to try it. My brother, Howard, was not very interested in the idea, but we decided to try it on fifteen acres.

The Wonder Life Company had a program and recommended that a chisel plow be used instead of a regular moldboard plow and that a soil inoculant be used, which helped get the soil back in condition. The first spring after we had used the soil inoculant we noticed lots of angle worms again. The way we had been farming, using the chemical fertilizers, few could be found, even though we never had used any insecticides.

We kept increasing the number of acres cropped with this new program, even though my brother was not too interested. Our yields were not as big as when we used chemical fertilizers, but our costs were lower. The soil improved in texture, too, and became more like a sponge, taking less power to till. As a result, the farm ponds around the edge of the fields in the pasture started to dry up because the rains would soak in, rather than run off.

One drawback we discovered was when chopping corn in the fall to fill silo, we could only fill the wagons half full because they would sink into the mellow soil and we would be stuck. My son, Andy, was big enough by this time to pull loads to the silo, and when he came home one evening from helping our neighbor fill silo, I asked him if he had problems pulling in the loads of silage. He replied, "Dad, their fields are just like concrete. Never got stuck once." Our neighbors had been using lots of fertilizers, herbicides, and insecticides, and the wagon tires only made prints on the soil.

About this time my brother Howard's two boys were out of high school, and we decided to divide the partnership. When we divided up the farmland, I got one hundred and eighty acres next to the home farm, and got to rent the home farm, which is three hundred and fifty-five acres. The farm is owned by my brother, sister, and me.

For the next six years I didn't use any chemical fertilizer or herbicides, and I had good crops. Once while I was getting the strips evened out to the same number of acres, I did something I was told not to do. I put one strip back to corn for the second year. It was a failure. The corn didn't grow good and the weeds came. I chopped it for silage, but there wasn't a good ear of corn in the field. Since that time, I have used some organic fertilizer, which helps get the corn up and out of the ground sooner so I can cultivate. I do use a small amount of herbicide if we get a rainy spring, and I can't get out to cultivate.

All the new equipment and devices to make work easier on the farm have a price tag attached. As I look to the future with my farming operation, I can see the day when I will have to decide either to borrow huge sums of money to purchase replacements for worn-out equipment, or quit farming altogether. I've been getting along by purchasing used equipment and repairing it, but even this old used equipment is getting scarce and the price is getting higher because of the high cost of new equipment.

My 4020 John Deere that I purchased new in 1964 has ninety-five horse power and cost $4,700. Today a new John Deere tractor with the same horse power costs $42,000. My round hay baler cost $3,100 in 1972; the same baler today has a price tag of $26,000. The field chopper which cost $1,800 new in 1956, costs $26,000 today.

I have been getting along with my old equipment because I have a small farm, and I make most of the parts for this old machinery when it breaks. I have to, because most repair parts are not available any more from the machinery dealer.

If I could only get a fair price for all the food I produce, I could make some machinery purchases which would help the hometown people and would put many people back to work in the factories again.

High Interest Dilemma

by Barb Leppert

The hardest thing for me to understand when we were first married and raising our family was the high interest. Every year when we'd figure taxes, I'd say, "Bob, look how much money we could have in the bank if we didn't have all that interest to pay."

He'd say, "Yes, Barb, but we have to borrow money to pay bills until we sell the cattle. We can't just let those people we owe wait for their money."

We were not into dairy then. We had a big check once a year when we sold cattle but by the time we paid off the bank loan and the interest, we were right back where we started. In a few weeks, Bob would come in and say, "Well, we need this or that and we don't have the money in the farm account to pay for it."

I'd think, "Here we go again. Just once I wish we could be out of debt."

It wasn't until thirty years later that I finally realized that dream. Our kids were grown up and gone from home by that time, but they were as happy as we were when we paid off the bank.

Bob's brother, Howard, and he were in partnership with their dad so everything was on thirds. Because our cash on hand was so minimal, we lived on a third of the egg check, which varied from $5 to $25 a week. From that money we bought things that we couldn't raise ourselves. We had our own meat, eggs, milk, and canned or frozen vegetables. Believe it or not, I was even able to save a few dollars out of our third each week until we had enough to go out for a special treat with our four children.

Life might have gone on this way for years, but my teaching certificate had to be renewed by the next year, because I had graduated in 1955 and mine was a ten-year certificate. I had to get six hours of credit in my chosen field. I went to summer school with a group of teachers from the local school system. Toward the end of the summer, they mentioned how much good substitute teachers were needed. They encouraged me to apply. I talked it over with Bob and my mother-in-law, who lived across the road from us. She and my sister, who lived in Lansing, would babysit our children. The substitute pay was $15 a day. I gave the babysitter $3 of that.

The next year a fourth-grade position opened up. The salary was $4,500 a year. To us that sounded like a fortune. Our oldest child was in the first grade and our youngest was just two years old when I started back teaching. The thing I liked most about this profession was that I was home at the same time as the kids. We had the same vacations and everything. Bob always said the money I made teaching helped keep our heads above water.

We have had to borrow money from time to time since, but it doesn't seem to be as threatening to me now. I am still teaching, and Bob gets half of the milk check every two weeks, so we can pretty much stay on top of things.

ESSIE WELSH

After helping with farm work and raising eight children, Essie entered college, earned her L.P.N. degree, and now works part-time in a nursing home. Like many others in the workshop, she surprised herself and pleased the rest of us with what she wrote..

Getting Started

As our farming career was about to begin, I saw that our major assets were our hopes, our dreams, our faith in God, a lot of ambition, and family support. Bill's only possession was a 1953 Chevy, and I had nothing but a small savings account. I was working in the office of a local factory, and Bill was working in a gas station just to get by until we could start farming.

Bill used his free time to go to farm sales, hoping to find the bargains and buy some of the essential farm equipment we would need. Then moving day came. Our household furnishings consisted of wedding gifts, family extras, and a new refrigerator—one with a foot pedal to open the door. Our local implement-appliance dealer said it hadn't been a big seller, so we got a bargain. A big, rusty, round oak stove, standing near the back entrance was to provide our heat. As the March winds blew through the house and water began to freeze in the kitchen sink, we came to realize that we needed another source of heat. We merely mentioned to my dad that our water pipes had frozen and that we even had ice in the dish pan. Soon we had an oil burner that they weren't using. Oh, how nice it was to be warm again!

For early spring field work we borrowed a tractor, a plow, a disc, and a planter, either from Bill's family or mine. We planted a garden, but I know we harvested more out of our parents' gardens than we did our own, and much of it came in jars.

Money was always in short supply and the cupboards were often pretty bare. Oatmeal was our staple. We didn't have a lot, but we didn't have much debt, either. When our first load of pigs was ready for market, we planned our first celebration. We invited Bill's brother, Dan, and his wife, Sarah, to have supper with us. All four of us squeezed into the cab of the pickup and took the pigs to market, then went to buy groceries for our celebration. We bought a chicken, potatoes for french fries, and bakery bread. We all worked together to cook supper. It was a fabulous meal. I can taste it yet.

In time, the rented farm where we began our career was sold, so we moved to the farm where we live today. This farm was owned by my uncle, Bill, and he had been renting the farm because of failing health. Now that we had more land, we bought more cows, and more feed. A brand new John Deere 60 tractor was delivered, which cost us $2,215.00. To us that was a lot of money at that time, a major debt, but this past year a major tractor repair cost over $5,000. By the time we bought the cattle, the feed, and the tractor, we were well indoctrinated into the process and need to borrow money. When I would get nervous and wonder how we were ever going to pay that money back, Bill would re-assure me by saying, "You can't start farming without borrowing money." Oh, how true that was and still is!

Our record keeping was simple those first years. Unlike my uncle, who kept his receipts in a shoe box and recorded checks and deposits on a long stick and merely got another when the first one got filled, we tried to keep a record of all farming and household income and expenses. We find those records interesting yet today. For example, in 1955 we paid $193.80 for a new foot pedal refrigerator, $25.80 for a used wringer washing machine, and $9.15 for a pair of bib overalls for Bill—the same brand that cost $21 to $23 today. That same year, market pigs brought $15 per hundred weight; today we are getting $40 to $43 per hundred weight. Prices have increased, but so have costs, so it seems we merely handle more money.

As time goes by, our hopes and dreams may change a bit, our ambition may fade, but we continue to see God in the things we do and in the people we meet, and we know that we all need one another.

The Coming Of Machinery

by Barb Leppert

With the coming of the age of machinery came long hours in the fields and consequently the loss of yet another old and valued tradition...that of visiting neighbors.

When there were only horses to pull the machinery, farmers could only work just so many hours, and then the horses had to be rested. The chores were done at the same time every night, and that left ample time after supper to go visit a close neighbor for the evening to play cards or whatever. It was fun. You never knew when someone would pop in, but it seemed like you always had some fixin's in the refrigerator for lunch.

Now when the field work starts you might see your husband at mealtime, unless he decides to take a sandwich and an apple along to the field with him, in which case you will only see him for five minutes when he comes in, washes up, and falls inito bed exhausted. He falls asleep two minutes after his head hits the pillow, so if you have anything you want to talk over with him, you'd better talk fast.

This ritual goes on during the planting, cultivating, and harvesting seasons. Then one day you come home from work and he's sitting on the steps with a big smile on his face and he says, "I'm done with the first crop hay. Let's celebrate and go out to eat. Why don't you call Betty and Curt and Donald and Eleanora and see if they want to go along?"

That's about as close to the old time visits as we get anymore. But that's the price we pay for progress!

Would You Believe It?

by Richard Sandry

Saturday afternoon, and it has been a beautiful day. The sun has shone all day, the humidity is low, and it's the kind of a day when you can look around and enjoy the beauty of all of the surrounding hills.

I am sitting in my combine, really enjoying my job. Everything is running smooth as silk. In about an hour I will be done for the season. I think it would be a good evening to go home, take a shower, and take my wife out for the evening meal. My thoughts are momentarily interrupted by a small squeaking noise. Well, I think, that can't be too serious. But soon I find I was very wrong, as within seconds the small squeak turns into a big squeak, then a loud bang, and right before my eyes the large auger on the header has just twisted into two pieces.

This means hundreds of dollars in repairs again, something we sure didn't need. Instead of that relaxing evening I had planned, we decide to save the money and figure out what to do next. After a night's sleep we decide to try to find someone willing to finish the field and postpone the repairs until next year.

Monday afternoon brings straw baling and again everything is humming along fine. One more load, I tell my son, and we will be done. He takes the previous load to the barn to unload, and I start on the final one. After about ten bales the pickup on the baler stops turning, something has broken inside. I take the baler to the machine shed and tell my son to go get the big baler and finish with that.

He is just about done when I see him stop. Upon inspection we find that a bearing on the big baler has "gone out." So much for that. This leaves a windrow of straw about fifty feet long in the field.

In relating this story to a friend I tell him that we were going to take the pitchfork and pick up the rest of the straw. "I wouldn't do that," he says. "You probably will break the fork handle."

GREG WELSH

Greg is an all-rounder who can run farm machinery, a food co-op, cook a meal for eight, garden, and write impressively. A man of ideas and energy, he has lived in urban areas, but returned to Lansing to live and work.

Forced Auctions

They gathered at the auction, harmless buzzards, strangers, neighbors, friends, relatives, patiently waiting, watching as the farmer's lifelong collection is sold.

"All right boys, what do ya want to give for it boys?" the auctioneer spouted, as the disc, plow, wagons, and tools sold to the highest bidders. Children wandered about, oblivious to the liquidation of their future.

Forced auctions, like an Irish wake, finality on the one hand, a neighborly respect to those passing on the other. No one asks why. It hurts too much. No one denies, it wouldn't be right.

Farm Crisis

by Greg Welsh

Through the eighties, each day the evening news reported a crisis still lived. A farm crisis, a human crisis, soundbites of emotional turmoil, forced auctions, and white crosses. A time of desperation, marked by suicides and fear, unnoticed by most.

The daily newspaper reported farm suicides and rural stress like that day's fatal car wreck, corporate buy-out, or weather.

What happened to agrarian wisdom? There's an auction, and another, and another. One more farmer sells, then another, and another. Then what? Then what?

The Tornado

by Frances Geinzer

May 22, 1962 is one of the days in my life I will never forget. It started like any other day with our morning chores. It was corn planting time, and my husband went to plant early that morning on one of our far back farms about two miles from home. Around noon the weather became very hazy and sultry and very still. We all kept working at our daily chores, but my mother said, "Start your chores and milking early, something bad is coming out of this weather." She was always afraid of us being in the barn when it was storming.

Well I, my aunt, and the man who was working for us got done and were out of the barn by 6:30 p.m. The sky was threatening and so dark and hazy. We all went to the house for supper. My husband was home from corn planting by then.

Well, after supper we done up the dishes and about 9 p.m. everybody was heading for bed but me. I had a bowl of gold fish and started cleaning them. I went outside to throw out the bowl of water and rain drops like spoonfuls and very hot were coming down, and it was so dark you could not see the hand before your face. I hurried inside, and just as I came through the door a gust of wind blew dirt right behind me. I rushed to the stairs and called to the folks to run for the cellar, something was going to happen. Well, we did. I was the last one down the stairs and could see through a window. Everything got real bright and it sounded like a freight train was going through the yard. Well, that is when it struck, then all got deathly quiet.

We finally went upstairs and rain was coming down the back stairway, a window was blew out and we got a big piece of cardboard to nail over it. Well, then mother looked out of her bedroom window, and that is when the nightmare began. Everything looked bare outside. We could see lights we never could see before.

I and my husband went outside and had to walk through the front yard as all the electric wires lay in the yard. The windmill lay only a foot from hitting the house. Our red barn was flat, tree limbs all over, pigs were squealing and calves were bellowing. The only light we had was in the house, all the others were out. Mother called some of the neighbors and one came over. We worked with the power saw freeing calves and two Angus bulls we had just bought. One had his leg injured and had to be sold, five calves were dead, as well as one sow and many young pigs. A sheep had a foot cut off and some geese were killed.

Well, when daylight came we found we had lost seven buildings. Our sheep shed we never did find. And everything had damage to some extent, except our tool shed and two brood coops full of young chickens. Seems crazy, but by 11 p.m. the stars were out. It was a beautiful night. Next day, lot of folks helped salvage things from the wreckage. Our milk cows got so frightened they took out a section of cowyard fence and we didn't find them until the next day. A system to milk them was set up in the old barn and we struggled with that all summer. By August a new barn was up and slowly we got back to normal, but no one knows what cleaning up after a tornado is like until they go through it. I know I will never forget.

DOROTHY SANDRY

Although Dorothy only showed up at the workshop once, when she wrote this piece, we have a hunch she'll be back again. After all, she did revise it for this book. She is shy, but with "Bluebirds" shows us a little part of herself.

Bluebirds

I have always enjoyed watching birds since grade school days when my teacher hung a bird feeder outside the window of our country school.

Some years ago in the spring, my husband came in from the pasture and told me he had seen a big flock of bluebirds. He made two houses and hung them for me. We watched and waited but no bluebirds came. The years went by and every so often I'd read more information on bluebirds.

About six years ago we decided to try again. We made eight new houses and hung them along our country road. I'll never forget one forenoon I heard a bird singing, and I came and looked out the kitchen window, and there sat a bluebird on the framework of my bird feeding station. Most of our houses were occupied by bluebirds that year.

We enjoyed it so much that the following winter we made more houses, so we now have twenty-four, which I check every seven to ten days, and record how many eggs each nest has, how many hatch, and how many fledge. Each fall I report these figures to a volunteer of the Department of Natural Resources.

Since the bluebird was on the endangered species list, they keep records from anyone who will report to them.

Since the decline of people using wooden fence posts, the bluebirds lost a lot of their nesting places. They are increasing in numbers now due to people and organizations putting up houses for them.

I really look forward to making the rounds of our bluebird trail. If my husband has time he joins me, for he enjoys it nearly as much as me. One year we recorded a bluebird nest with pictures, beginning with the eggs and ending with the young birds nearly ready to fly. The mother bird was very protective of her eggs, so we also got a picture of her sitting on the nest.

We can often look out onto our lawn and see one bluebird or several at our birdbath or on the lawn looking for insects.

We have learned so much since we put up those first two houses years ago. The biggest problem we had was that something was getting into the nest and pulling it apart, destroying the eggs. Often we'd find adult feathers laying on the ground. For several years we lost a lot of nestings. Finally we figured the culprit was a raccoon. I made a phone call to an Urban Nongame Biologist with the DNR and she sent me information on what to do.

One suggestion was to put several small dowels on the inside front of the house a little way down from the entrance hole. The idea was that the dowels would stop anything from being pulled up toward the hole. That did not work. So next I made a hardware cloth cone measuring three and a half inches wide, five inches tall, that extended six inches out from the box. This was stapled onto the front of the house over the hole. We bent the outer prongs of the hardware cloth out so there was a sharp edge all the way around.

Success at last! Last year we had no more problems with the raccoon. We fledged eighty-six bluebirds and are looking forward to their return this spring.

PART III:

LAND STEWARDSHIP

BRUCE CARLSON

Bruce is a dentist who works conscientiously on local community projects. In his free time, depending on the season, he gardens, bikes, skates, or skiis. He also practices zazen, or Zen meditation.

Soil

I was not raised on a farm, but farming and the soil have been a part of my life. Living on the world's largest fertile plain has had an impact on me. The texture and feel of soil in my hands has been a powerful connection to the environment for me since I was a boy working in my parents' garden.

I was raised in Ames, Iowa, home of Iowa State University, one of the original land grant colleges. These institutions have shaped farming practices for over a hundred years. In the late sixties and early seventies, when our society was in turmoil, the government and these agricultural institutions felt the need to expand U.S. agricultural exports to feed the world and bolster our economy. Farming techniques that had been evolving for centuries were put aside and the genetic engineering of seeds and the heavy use of chemicals became the way.

Looking back, if we would have developed sustainable agricultural technologies for export, the world's food supply would be light years ahead of where it is today.

To save and build the soils we have left, is what organic farming is about. There were a few farmers who followed their instincts and never left crop rotations, wind breaks, and the many practices that farming fence-to-fence with lots of chemicals and big equipment seemed to make passé. It must be hard to be a sustainable farmer and see the majority of your colleagues throwing chemicals everywhere and reaping short-term profits from exploiting the land.

The turmoil between generations that the sixties produced was very evident in organic farming. It seemed that organic farmers were hippies with long, dirty hair living in a commune. This image was promoted to the point where it would have been un-American to see any value in anything these people believed in.

If the universities had promoted the values of the Aldo Leopold Center for Sustainable Agriculture, instead of following the advice of pro-chemical lobbyists, like the former Secretary of Agriculture Earl Butz, the hippies would have only been on the fringe for their lifestyles, not their farming practices.

To see the corruption and greed of corporate America creep into our soils has been hard for me. When I watch soil run thick as chocolate down an erosion rill, I am sickened. Taking for granted and abusing this precious ingredient to life is a sin. I find it hard to believe that even a hundred years ago, when soils were so thick it seemed they could not be depleted, that a farmer would not have been saddened to see the destruction of his fields from the power of one rain storm.

We speak of tolerable soil loss. Why do we farm on a limited and depletable medium and speak of its demise as tolerable? Why do we tolerate non-sustainable agriculture?

I have lived on the banks of the Mississippi River for fourteen years. The power that a river is, the energy in moving water, may be why I love this ecosystem so much. The soils from the hills that surround this mother of all rivers have literally been choking the life out of the water.

The realization that farming practices are the reason for the river's demise has been hard for me. I've always felt the Corps of Engineers was the dirty culprit by diverting as much water as possible away from the backwaters into the main channel. To see chemically laden silt choking these backwaters is wrong, yet we have done almost nothing to stop the practice of tolerable soil loss that has led to the depletion of life within this river's ecosystem.

I feel the way we treat our soil is so indicative of how we feel about our planet and the ecosystem we live in. Could it be that if we changed our thinking about soil loss *not* being tolerable, air and water pollution *not* being tolerable, human suffering and corporate greed *not* being tolerable, that all life on earth would be sustainable?

Image of Farmers

by Essie Welsh

My mental picture of a farmer is a man dressed in bib overalls or blue jeans, a chambray or flannel shirt, sturdy high top shoes and a hat that advertises for the local machine or seed dealer. He carries a pencil and a small notebook in his pocket to help him remember appointments, record the number of pigs per litter, the date a new calf was born, or the variety of seed he planted on the west side of the road and in the terraced piece.

Today we commonly see pictures of farmers wearing one-piece coveralls, plastic gloves, plastic boots, and plastic eye protection. That is what he needs to wear to reduce his exposure to chemicals—those same chemicals that we apply to the land which directly produces the food we eat or produces the feed for our animals, which will eventually provide the food we eat.

Is this a sign of advanced technology in the clothing industry? Is this advancement in agriculture, or suicide for healthy family life?

What about that farmer in his overalls and chambray shirt who for years applied those same chemicals to his land without the protection of the spacesuit-type wardrobe; who ate his lunch in the fields with the same unprotected hands that had handled the chemicals as they were being mixed and applied to the land?

What about the nine-year-old boy who spent five days of his summer vacation in the hospital, desperately sick with high fever, swelling and extensive rash that was diagnosed as an acute inflammatory disease (Erythema Multiforme), cause unknown?

What about the farmer whose hands and arms swell every spring while he is applying chemicals?

What about the farmer who grows his crops without using synthetic chemicals, yet watches the chemical drift travel through the air as his neighbor's corn field is being sprayed with a herbicide by a hired commercial sprayer because he doesn't have time or doesn't want to cultivate?

What about the cost to that farmer who pays for commercial spray application but loses valuable product to the atmosphere as the country breezes carry it through the air?

Yes, we farm men and women are always looking for new technology to save time and make farm work easier, but how much are we willing to pay? How much are we willing to sacrifice? How long are we going to ignore the research that assures us there are alternatives?

BILL WELSH

In June 1991, when I was first looking for farmers for this project, especially farmers with an interest in land stewardship, Bruce Carlson recommended Bill Welsh, an organic farmer. In September I met Bill, Essie, and Greg on one of their farm tours. Bill, who bears a striking resemblance to Grant Wood, is a bespectacled, nearly stout man with a keen sense of humor, almost always dressed in bib overalls.

The Day the Welsh Family Farm Turned Around

Friday, May 10th, 1981, is a day that I will always remember. My day started at sun-up. It was corn planting time in Iowa, which means long days in the fields. We started with chores at the home place and figured out how we could make the best use of the day. A bit of anxiety was pushing us because the following day, at noon, we were to leave for Dubuque to attend the college graduation ceremonies for our eldest son, Greg. We decided that I would start planting, while Gary went to the other farm, "Pat's," as it was called, to feed the cows.

I had just pulled into the field with the corn planter when I saw Gary racing to the field where I was working. I knew as soon as I saw him coming that something was very wrong. When he got to where I was, he jumped out of the pickup and hollered, "Come quick, the cows at Pat's are crazy!" We rushed to get over there, stopping at the house only long enough to call the vet.

As we arrived at Pat's, the first thing I saw was one cow lying dead. As I walked into the lot where the cows were, one of my favorite cows took after me and chased me over the fence. I remember thinking, what in the world is wrong with her! She was always such a gentle animal. Then we noticed three more dead cows piled on top of one another in the corner of the fence and the others running, as hard as they could, around the lot. Soon the vet arrived and he immediately said, "They are being poisoned by something."

A search began to find the source. We looked, we thought, and we looked some more. We found nothing. Soon four other veterinarians arrived to help. Brothers and neighbors were called to help, and in less than an hour the yard was full of cars. The search continued for a cause, but nothing was found.

The veterinarians decided we just had to start getting the cows into a catch chute so they could be injected with an antidote. Someone went to get the chute, others went after gates to make a runway to guide the cattle into the chute. At the same time, it was decided that one of the dead cows should be sent to a diagnostic lab. The nearest lab was contacted, and they said they would be glad to do the testing, but due to the fact that it was Friday, they could not get at it until Monday. Nevertheless, my brother Bernard was chosen for that task. Someone else went to get a manure loader to hoist the cow into the back of his pickup. Bernard immediately left for Madison, Wisconsin with a dead cow laying in the back of his pickup with all four feet in the air.

Bernard tells the story that when he got to Madison, he wasn't sure how to get to the laboratory. He saw two young men standing on the street corner, so decided to ask them for directions. As he approached them he decided it would be more fun to ask, "Where's the closest McDonald's?"

At Pat's, the job of putting the cows into the chute began. We were told that this would have to be done every four hours for at least forty-eight to seventy-two hours, maybe longer. Plans started developing on who was going to help with each succeeding shift so that we would have enough help to get through the night. The cows moved into the chute fairly easy the first trip, but each succeeding time it became more and more difficult, until at last, we were literally carrying some of them. Each time we put them through the chute, more had died.

Sometime in the afternoon, between "chute jobs," I was sitting on the fence, still trying to figure out what had happened. Then I remembered, there was a bale of hay that the cows were not eating. I had told Gary the day before that he should not give them more new hay until they had cleaned that bale up. I started wondering where that bale had come from and Gary remembered exactly, because there were very few bales left in the shed. We all went to the hay shed and soon found the problem. We found parts of a decomposed paper Dyfonate bag (an insecticide used for rootworm control) laying on the floor where that bale had been. Going back to the feeder where the refused hay bale was, we found parts of the same Dyfonate bag. The mystery was solved.

We continued to give the cows their antidote shots every four hours. Between each exhausting session, I felt very troubled about whether or not to try and go to Greg's graduation the following day. The decision was tearing my guts out. I had often dreamed about the day Greg would graduate from college, now would I even be able to go?

I spent the night in the barn, getting only a few minutes of sleep while lying on a bale of straw. This was probably the longest night of my life. By morning, the decision to go to graduation seemed much easier, probably because I was too tired to argue with my son, Gary, my brothers, and my neighbors, who had been telling me all along that they would take care of things.

At noon we left for Dubuque. I still wondered if I was doing the right thing. The time spent in Dubuque seems hazy. All I really remember was how proud I was of Greg for accomplishing something I had never been able to do.

When we returned home Sunday evening, I went straight to Pat's to check on the cows. By now thirteen had died. Soon the vet arrived again. They had decided at noon that day to discontinue the antidote shots because they really weren't sure if the last cows had died from the poison or from the antidote. The vet and I sat on the fence that evening and talked for a long time. He told me that a tablespoon of the insecticide, Dyfonate, spread evenly enough throughout the bale, could have killed all those cows and that if we used five pounds of it per acre for twenty years we would have one hundred pounds of it somewhere in our environment. It might be disbursed, washed away by rains into nearby ponds, creeks, rivers, and eventually into the ocean, but it would always be somewhere. It is not biodegradable. It was in this discussion that I first realized that the chemicals we were using in farming were the same ones used in chemical warfare that I had learned about years before as an instructor in atomic, biological, and chemical warfare during my tour of duty in the Air Force. Frankly, that scared the hell out of me. I vowed that Sunday evening that never again would I use that product or anything like it on any land that I owned.

That is when the search for ways to farm without chemicals began. We didn't know where or how to start, but were convinced that we had to find a way. Planting time, 1982, became a real nightmare. We were unsure of what to plant where, or what to try first, but we were positively sure we would not use any more insecticide. Some of our crops that year were not that great, but we were learning and became confident we could do better next year.

The Way Back

by Greg Welsh

"Sometimes you have to go a long distance out of your way to come back a short distance correctly."
—Edward Albee

I grew up on a farm in northeast Iowa, the eldest son of eight children, nurtured by my father's pride and embraced by the land. But eventually everyone needs something of his own, a sense of who he is. Trying to find mine, I rejected a proud father and the vulnerable land, and I learned a lot about selfishness, anger, loneliness, before my search brought me back to where I started. I don't know if I'll ever find that elusive self I was after, but I may have found a crucial part of it in what I tried to leave behind.

My first eight years on the farm were magical. Each day brought with it its own adventure, the fascination at the birth of a calf, a new corner of the hay barn to explore in awe. And the crazy yearning, the consuming hunger to operate the machinery. I remember how my brother, Gary, and I planned for weeks the best way to ask Dad if we could drive the tractor in third gear. After a fairly extensive safety speech, he, miraculously, said yes. You've never seen two happier boys.

But few idylls last forever, and never those that begin when we're young. Third gear advanced to road gear, and I began a spiral of personal disillusion and dissatisfaction about the same time Earl Butz began in earnest his assault on the land and the American family farm. Expansion, yield, fence-row to fence-row production, "feed the world."

We rented more land, poured on fertilizer and pesticides, tried for that ultimate yield. Chores now were done with syringe in hand. Dead livestock no longer phased me at all. It seemed normal. The veterinarian almost lived with us. He sent us his bill as we buried the animals. We were farming by the book, and it was tearing our family apart.

It was a question both of "too much" and "too little." Too much productivity that meant too much work, too much debt, too much anger, with too little return, too little communication, too little time for love. I was old enough to know there was more than one right way, and I had ideas of my own. But my father didn't seem capable of listening. He only seemed capable of working hard. I hated him for working so stubbornly hard.

In contrast, town kids had it made. No chores to speak of. They could play baseball whenever they wanted. Often I would stay overnight with friends in town, but seldom asked friends to come to the farm. I told my mother they wouldn't have any fun. I was in high school, and I was ashamed of the farm, my family, my life.

I longed, vaguely but completely, to make a difference, and it seemed clear that I couldn't do so at home. So I dreamed of escape: to college, to law school, to a time when I could exist on my own terms, without the stigma of where I'd come from and who I'd been.

In college I got to be a town kid. I missed calving in the spring, the planting, the field work. I missed harvest. I would go back to the farm gladly on vacation. But the romance was short-lived each time, and I was equally glad to leave again. I never gave a thought to returning for good to the embrace the land held me in as a child.

While I was at college, nothing every really replaced my love for my family. But that love did take some curious turns. Naively, I picturely myself a successful lawyer with enough money to help them out of their mounting debt. I pictured them loving me finally for what I'd made of myself. I pictured myself recognized. But I never pictured myself sharing my life with them steadily, completely, as I had before and as many rural families still do.

As for my father, I felt sorry for him. Because he was still on the farm. Because he was still working hard. Because he still didn't know what I already was sure of.

My world expanded with each new possibility, each new friend, each new bit of knowledge I acquired, even as it shrank from the lack of intimacy with the people and things that formed my heart as I grew up. After a close college friend met my parents at graduation, he turned and said to me, "I didn't know you came from a farm." Somehow I'd forgotten to tell him. Somehow I'd forgotten.

Then, in the spring of 1981, an incident occurred which I see now as the beginning of my gradual return to the love of both my father and the land, love I had always needed and will never outgrow. A year earlier, at planting time, an empty bag of Dyfonate insecticide had been overlooked and left on the floor of our hay shed. A little later, the shed was filled with large, round bales of hay, which during the year we fed to our cattle.

Now, after a whole year, the bale of hay that had been on top of the empty Dyfonate bag had absorbed enough residual pesticide to poison forty full-grown pregnant cows. Thirteen eventually died. It didn't take a college education to realize there was something incredibly wrong with what had happened. I was outraged. Why were we permitted to buy such toxic products? Why were they allowed to be on the market in the first place? And what about the six to ten pounds per acre of Dyfonate that we and a large percentage of farmers like us used each year to control rootworms? What had it already done, what was it still doing, to our soil, our water, our food, ourselves?

The experience shattered my father's rigid views of farming. He swore he'd never use chemicals again. He found a reason to fight, to believe, a reason for more than stubborn work. He opened, grew, rediscovered discovery. He became approachable. I saw that he could see me, hear me again. I saw there could be a way.

But I wasn't ready. For four years I had pursued other dreams, had tested other environments, and they weren't so easily abandoned. I spent the winter working in Corpus Christi, Texas. I kept in touch with my professors, applied to law schools. I knew what I wanted.

In Texas I developed a condition I convinced myself was cancer. And why not cancer? Look at what the Dyfonate had done to our cattle. I remembered how, in high school, the daughter of a neighboring farmer was diagnosed with cancer. Cancer seemed to me the logical, horrifying inheritance of farm families, the deadly bequest of chemical agriculture.

Suddenly my life seemed so very short, my accomplishments so very few. I'd made no difference, I would never make a difference. I was angry, frightened, lonely. I was dying.

I went home.

It took about two months for the official verdict to come in. Expecting the worst, I cried all the way to the doctor. But I did not have cancer. I had a serious infection, but it could be cured completely and fairly quickly with antibiotics. I had gotten a stay of execution. The relief was amazing. So was the feeling of stupidity. My imagination surprised me.

Nothing really changed. And everything did. If my cancer wasn't real, the threat of cancer to myself, my family, my neighbors still was. The economics of overproductive agribusiness threatened a whole way of life, *my* way of life, despite the years I tried to deny it. And the chemical dependency at the heart of that economics threatened not only the lives of farm families, but of anyone eating the food farms produced, or drinking water from contaminated aquifers.

I, too, rediscovered discovery.

Of course transformations are never really instantaneous. After every turning point there are residues left of our former selves that only patience can eradicate. For awhile I became a self-righteous environmentalist, the most righteous environment-alist in the county for sure. I was intolerant of the sheer blockheadedness of many farmers in the light of my new found truth. There were still heated arguments with my father, despite our similar views.

It was clear to me that the natural, organic life of the soil was a slow, dynamic process never to be completed. But it took much longer for me to see that the inner lives of men and women, my father's and my own included, are similar processes.

It seems to me now the true quality of both the soil and the spirit, of all life, should not be judged on what it is at any given moment, like a finished product, but should be loved for the emergent things they are. It seems to me now that all things are continually making themselves and each other. And there seems little need for amends. Everything—the crops, the laughter in my father's eyes—is reconciliation.

I am always amazed at the amount of life in the soil, at the resiliency of it, and I am convinced we should do nothing to destroy its creative ability. And I am amazed, too, at the life, love, and resiliency in my father's heart and, to my surprise, in my own. I'm amazed and afraid, and I pray I will soon cease doing anything that might endanger that creativity.

FREE RIVER PRESS
Folk Literature Series

Ancient Chinese emperors maintained a Music Bureau, whose function was to collect folk songs from across the empire. By these songs the emperor sought to know whether a local government functioned well, whether a duke or prince performed his duties, and whatever else might be on the people's minds.

The Free River Press folk literature series is a modest imitation of the Music Bureau. Its writings are mostly generated in Free River Press writing workshops. To date the press has worked with the homeless and with farmers, but eventually will work with Americans of all social standings and a diversity of occupations. The press hopes that thirty years hence the folk literature series will resemble a collective autobiography of America.

Free River Press Folk Literature Series:

Robert Wolf, ed. **Five Street Poets.** $4.95
Robert Wolf, ed. **Passing Thru.** $4.95
El Gilbert. **Lion's Share.** $4.95
Josef Goller. **From within Walls.** $4.95
Diana Schooler. **Lemme Tell You where I Used to Live.** $4.95
Rebel Yell. **Hitchhiker's Dream.** $4.95
Robert Wolf, ed. **Voices from the Land.** $4.95